Cornerstones of Freedom

The Story of
LEXINGTON
AND
CONCORD

By R. Conrad Stein

Illustrated by Keith Neely

 CHILDRENS PRESS, CHICAGO

Library of Congress Cataloging in Publication Data

Stein, R. Conrad.
  The story of Lexington and Concord.

  (Cornerstones of freedom)
  Summary: Discusses the causes and consequences of the
battles which marked the beginning of the American
revolution, in April 1775, after local militiamen were
warned by Paul Revere that British troops had set out
from Boston.
  1. Lexington, Battle of, 1775 — Juvenile literature.
2. Concord, Battle of, 1775 — Juvenile literature.
[1. Lexington, Battle of, 1775.   2.   Concord, Battle of,
1775.   3.   United States — History — Revolution, 1775-1783 —
Campaigns and battles.   4.   Revere, Paul, 1735-1818]
I. Title. II. Series.
E241.L6S75 1983   973.3'311   82-23518
ISBN 0-516-04661-6   AACR2

No one knows the name of the messenger who banged on Paul Revere's door in Boston on the night of April 18, 1775. No doubt the messenger said he was sent by Dr. Joseph Warren. And no doubt Revere hurried through the night streets to meet the doctor.

Paul Revere was a silversmith. His skilled hands had created some of the most beautiful silver teapots, cups, and goblets that could be found in the colonies. Joseph Warren was a respected doctor who had turned revolutionary. A British official once called him the "greatest incendiary in all America."

At the time, Boston was a city under siege. Sixteen months earlier, a group of angry Bostonians had dumped 342 chests of tea into the Boston Harbor. The group was protesting the British tax on tea. To punish the Bostonians, the king of England closed the Boston Harbor. He also sent 4,000 troops and a fleet of warships to the city. The king announced that the troops and the ships would remain until someone paid for the tea.

American spies in Boston kept track of the British troop movements. The spies determined that a large British force would soon leave Boston and march to the nearby cities of Lexington and Concord. Living in Lexington were two important revolutionary leaders, John Hancock and Samuel Adams. In Concord the colonists had hidden a cache of supplies to be used in case war broke out with England.

Huddled under a flickering lamp, Paul Revere and Joseph Warren spoke. Revere later wrote, "Dr. Warren. . . begged that I would immediately set out for Lexington, where Messrs. Hancock and Adams were, and acquaint them of the [British troop] movement. . . . I then went home, took my boots and surtout, went to the north part of town, where I had kept a boat."

With two friends Revere rowed across the Charles River. The moon was so bright that it cast shadows. The men had to steer dangerously close to the British warship *Somerset*, which drifted at anchor. To silence any squeaking, the rowers had torn up a woman's petticoat and stuffed the pieces into the oarlocks. The petticoat had been donated by one of Revere's neighbors.

That same evening, a second messenger galloped out of Boston. He was a plump young shoemaker named William Dawes, who was to meet Revere at Lexington.

A few days earlier, Revere had arranged a signal to let nearby patriots know how the British troops were planning to leave Boston. A friend would put one or two lanterns in the window of Boston's towering North Church. Two lanterns if the British left by boat. One if they left the city on foot.

On the night of April 18, two lanterns burned in the window high up in the church steeple. The British soldiers were preparing to leave Boston by boat.

After reaching Charlestown, on the other side of the Charles River, Paul Revere borrowed a horse from friends. He then thundered away on a ride that would carry him to fame. Many years later, poet Henry Wadsworth Longfellow immortalized Revere's dash to Lexington. His poem starts with these lines:

> Listen my children, and you shall hear
> Of the midnight ride of Paul Revere.

Dodging British patrols, Revere rushed over the Lexington road. The town was a twelve-mile ride

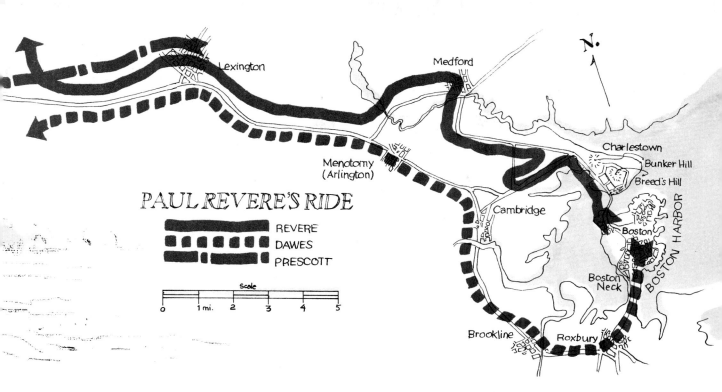

PAUL REVERE'S RIDE

REVERE
DAWES
PRESCOTT

Scale

0   1 mi.   2   3   4   5

from Charlestown. Revere was a splendid horseman and knew the tangle of roads that spread over the countryside. While galloping down the moonlit road, he shouted to the farmhouses that the British were on the move. He later said, "I alarmed almost every house, until I got to Lexington."

The people of Lexington already suspected trouble was brewing. They had posted guards around the house where John Hancock and Samuel Adams slept. One member of the guard was a soldier named William Munroe. He wrote, "About midnight, Colonel Paul Revere rode up and requested admittance. I told him the [people] had just retired, and had requested that they not be disturbed by any noise about the house.

" 'Noise!' said he. 'You'll have noise enough before long. The [British] regulars are coming out.' "

Revere stayed in Lexington long enough to persuade Hancock and Adams to leave the town. He then set out with two other riders to warn the town of Concord. Revere's companions were the shoemaker William Dawes and a young doctor named Samuel Prescott. Just minutes out of Lexington the three men ran into a British patrol. Revere was captured, but Dawes and Prescott escaped. The British finally let Revere go after taking his horse. So Paul Revere, the famed horseman of the poem, was forced to walk back to Lexington. William Dawes also returned to Lexington. But Dr. Samuel Prescott carried the alarm to Concord. He rode at breakneck speed through the night, shouting all the way that the British were coming.

Indeed the British *were* coming. Under the pre-dawn stars a force of seven hundred soldiers marched up to the tiny town of Lexington, Massachusetts.

As they marched, the British soldiers quickly realized that the colonists had been warned of their approach. Hours before sunrise, houses along the roadside were lit. In the distance, the soldiers heard church bells pealing. The regiment was commanded by Colonel Francis Smith. His orders read: "Sir. You will march. . . with the utmost secrecy to Concord where you will seize and destroy all the artillery and ammunition you can find." As the regiment approached Lexington, the whole town was stirring. Colonel Smith knew he had not achieved "the utmost secrecy."

Tensions between the colonies and the mother country were high. Still, neither side wanted to start a war on this April morning. Great Britain could not afford to fight a new foreign war. The British hoped only to destroy the colonists' secret cache of arms, and to frighten the Americans with the power of their army. One of the leaders of the British force was a major named Pitcairn. In a letter written before the march, he said, "I am satisfied that one active campaign, a smart action, and burning two or three of their towns, will set everything to rights." The colonists did not want war, either. Most of them believed they could continue to live under the British Crown as they had for more than a hundred years. Still, the colonists were determined to stand up to British might and prove they were not afraid of the British army.

The mood of the British troops was foul. They had been up all night wading through swamps and marching over dark roads. Now, wet, tired, and miserable, they cursed the day they first set eyes on the shores of America. Their anger increased as they streamed into Lexington and heard the rat-a-tat of a drummer beating the call to arms. In Lexington stood a rag-tag troop of about sixty colonists.

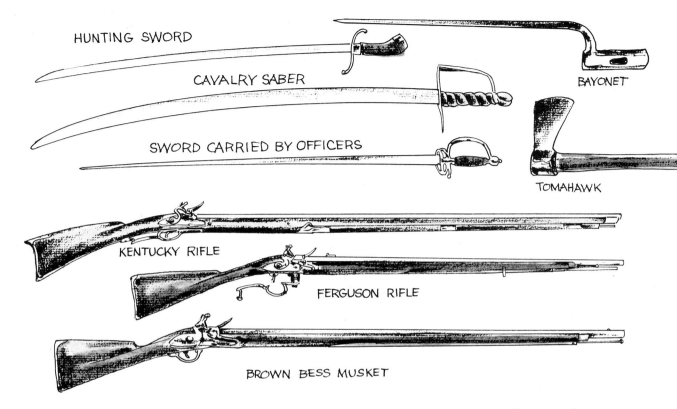

HUNTING SWORD

CAVALRY SABER

BAYONET

SWORD CARRIED BY OFFICERS

TOMAHAWK

KENTUCKY RIFLE

FERGUSON RIFLE

BROWN BESS MUSKET

Led by Captain John Parker, most were members of a group called the Minutemen. They claimed they could assemble and fight at a minute's notice. The Minutemen were armed with muskets, squirrel guns, and a bewildering assortment of other firearms.

Major Pitcairn commanded the forward units of the British forces. His orders were to avoid bloodshed with the colonists. Parker also had warned his men not to fire unless fired on. "But," he had said, "if they mean to have war, let it begin here."

The British marched to within a stone's throw of the line of Minutemen. There Major Pitcairn ordered his troops to halt. Several minutes of tense silence passed. Men on both sides glared at each other. Finally, Major Pitcairn demanded that the Minutemen surrender their rifles and go home. Not one of the colonists dropped his rifle. A few did shrug their shoulders and begin to walk away.

Suddenly a shot rang out. It was later called "the shot heard round the world." No one is sure who fired it. Later the Americans blamed the British and the British blamed the Americans.

The first shot was followed by the crackling of a dozen British muskets. Major Pitcairn bellowed for his men to stop. But the British soldiers continued shooting. Finally, the English major rode his horse in front of the ranks of soldiers, flashing his sword downward in a signal to cease fire. But the British troops continued to shoot at the Americans for five deadly minutes. A British lieutenant named Barker wrote, "The men were so wild they could hear no orders." Meanwhile, the woefully outnumbered Minutemen ran for their lives.

When the last puff of gunsmoke faded into the air, eight Minutemen lay dead on the grass. Ten others were wounded. One British soldier had been hit by a musket shot.

The battle at Lexington marked the start of an unbelievable April day. No one realized it at the time, but this small skirmish was the beginning of the American Revolutionary War.

The seeds of the American Revolution had been planted a dozen years earlier. In 1763, a long and bitter war between France and Great Britain ended. In Europe it was called the Seven Years' War. In the colonies it was called the French and Indian War. Great Britain won the war and became the supreme power in North America. France surrendered Canada and its territory in the Mississippi Valley. At first, the colonists rejoiced in victory along with their mother country. However, the victory set the stage for a violent family quarrel.

The war had cost the British enormous sums of money. England was deeply in debt. The country was ruled by King George III. He was honest, well-intentioned, and stubborn. To raise money to pay England's huge war debt, George III decided to tax the colonies. Never before had England levied severe taxes on her North American colonies. The colonists had no representatives in the British Parliament. So it was thought to be unfair to tax them. But someone had to pay England's war debt.

Suddenly a host of new taxes fell upon the colonists. Taxes were imposed on sugar, on tea, and on legal certificates called stamps. The colonists complained that these taxes were illegal because the colonies were not represented in Parliament. The cry "taxation without representation is tyranny" echoed throughout the land.

The king's taxes actually helped unify the colonies. Until then, the colonies had been divided into thirteen separate governing bodies. Each body was jealous of the others. Now the people's fury over taxation without representation drew the colonists together. Men and women who used to think of themselves as Virginians, New Yorkers, or Pennsylvanians suddenly began to believe they were something different, something new—Americans.

In every colony, groups formed to protest the taxes. At first, the groups demanded "the rights of Englishmen." That meant that they could not be taxed without having representatives in Parliament. Gradually, secret societies such as the Sons of Liberty began to whisper the word "independence." They claimed that George III and the British Parliament would never listen to the American colonists thousands of miles from London. Now, said many of the Sons of Liberty, was the time to establish a new country.

In Great Britain, George III became alarmed by the radical thinking in his prized colonies. He increased British troop strength in North America. The presence of troops invited clashes with the colonists. In 1770, a fistfight between a colonial workman and a British soldier mushroomed into what was later called the Boston Massacre. Five colonists were killed. An atmosphere of tension swept Boston. The tension led to the rise of armed groups such as the Minutemen. The armed groups began hiding caches of rifles and ammunition. The British army hoped to destroyed those hidden supplies. And for that reason, the British marched out of Boston toward Lexington and Concord on that fateful day, April 19, 1775.

In Lexington, British commander Smith felt like a man who had just kicked a hornet's nest. He knew the shooting would bring hundreds of colonists to the scene. So he sent messengers to Boston asking for reinforcements. He then ordered his men back on the road for the advance on Concord.

The British troops looked splendid marching in long ranks under the rising sun. The men wore white trousers and bright red jackets. The British army was famous for its iron discipline and cool courage under fire. Led by their mighty army, Great Britain had carved out an empire that was second in history only to that of ancient Rome. But the British soldiers were accustomed to fighting European wars. There, precise battle lines were drawn between foes. Attacks were made by troops marching smartly as if they were on a parade ground. The Americans, on the other hand, had learned their fighting from the

Indians. They believed in materializing out of a forest, striking their enemy, and melting back into the forest again.

At Concord, the warning that "the redcoats are coming" had been passed first by Prescott, and then by dozens of riders coming up from Lexington. Some 250 Americans had assembled under the command of Major John Buttrick. Many of them were Minutemen. Others were members of the colonial militia. This hurriedly formed army marched out to meet the British. Their fife players and drummers beat out a lively tune called "The White Cockade."

The Americans had gone about a mile down the road when they heard the sound of British fifes and drums. On the horizon they saw the vanguard of seven hundred British soldiers. A Minuteman named Thaddeus Blood remembered, "We... saw the British acoming.... The sun was rising and shined on their arms, and they made a noble appearance in their red coats and glistening arms."

When only two hundred yards separated the two armies, Buttrick ordered his men to halt. He then told the men to face about and march back to Concord. Clearly outnumbered, he had no desire to fight an entire British regiment. No shots were fired. No soldier made a wild dash at his enemy's ranks. Despite the blood spilled at Lexington, neither side wanted a war. So a curious parade marched back to Concord. First came the Americans, then the British. In the words of Minuteman Amos Barrett, "We... marched before them with our drums and fifes agoing, and also the British. We had grand music."

The British moved to the center of Concord, while the main body of Americans occupied a sandy hill near the town. Soldiers from each side tried to keep a respectful distance from the other. Some of the

British officers ordered breakfast at Wright's Tavern on the town square. They were careful to pay for everything they ate.

At once, the British began to search for the rifles and gunpowder the Americans had stored. They found practically nothing. During the night, the townspeople had moved most of the supplies to near-by patches of woods. The British did find a few small kegs of gunpowder. They threw some of it into a bonfire they had started near the town hall. The bonfire upset seventy-one-year-old Martha Moulton, who lived next door. "[I] ventured to beg of the officers to send some of their men to put out the fire; but they took no notice. . . ." said Mrs. Moulton. "They only said, 'O, mother, we won't do you any harm!' 'Don't be concerned, mother!' and such like talk."

The bonfire upset the Minutemen too. The billowing smoke could be seen plainly from the outskirts of town. There Americans had gathered in small groups. With each passing moment, the groups grew in numbers. From the fields and surrounding towns came farmers, storekeepers, and tradesmen. Many were veterans of the French and Indian War. Each of them carried some sort of firearm. As they

gathered, the mood of the Americans grew more and more uneasy.

Major Buttrick studied the black pillar of smoke curling from town. From where he stood, he had no idea if the smoke came from a bonfire or if the British had set Concord on fire. Suddenly a Concord man named Joseph Rosmer cried out, "Will you let them burn the town down?" The men shouted back, "No!" Major Buttrick led a force of about four hundred men toward Concord.

To enter the town, the Americans had to cross the North Bridge. A British unit moved quickly to prevent the crossing. Minuteman Amos Barrett said ". . . there was about eighty or ninety British came to the bridge and there made a halt. After a while they [the British] began to tear up the planks of the bridge. Major Buttrick said. . . he would drive them away from the bridge. They should not tear that up. We all said we would go."

In a column of twos, the Americans advanced toward the bridge. Their forward movement made the British soldiers tear up the planks even faster. Amos Barret wrote, "[we] had strict orders not to fire till they fired first." The British troops, too, had been told not to fire.

But, as at Lexington, a sudden shot rang out. It probably was fired from the British side. Witnesses claimed that after the first shot, Major Buttrick cried out, "Fire, fellow soldiers. For God's sake, fire!"

The Minutemen fired across the bridge into the crowded ranks of the redcoats. Three British soldiers were killed instantly. Eight to ten others fell wounded. The rest of the ninety or so redcoats ran back to the town square to join their main body.

The rag-tag Americans had forced a unit of the mighty British army to retreat.

The British commander now pondered what to do. Colonel Francis Smith was a fat, fussy man who made decisions only with great difficulty. His search for military supplies had yielded practically nothing. And the longer he waited, the stronger the American forces became. For miles in every direction, Americans were leaving their plows in the ground, grabbing rifles, and heading for Concord. Logically, Colonel Smith should have hurried back to Boston before he became outnumbered. Still, it took the colonel two hours to order his men to form ranks for the march back. By that time, both sides of the road to Boston were lined with American riflemen. One British soldier said the Americans seemed to "drop from the clouds."

With Colonel Smith leading the way on horseback, the British regiment started out of Concord. "The British marched down the hill with slow but steady steps, without music, or a word being spoken that could be heard," wrote American Edmund Foster. "Silence reigned on both sides. As soon as the British had gained the main road... they faced about suddenly and fired a volley of musketry upon us.

They overshot; and no one, to my knowledge, was injured by the fire. The fire was immediately returned by the Americans and two British soldiers fell dead."

The long British flight from Concord had begun. It was a march that no redcoat would ever forget.

Lurking in the woods, Indian-style, were American riflemen. Both sides of the road were covered. From behind a patch of trees or a scattering of boulders, a dozen rifle muzzles would suddenly poke out. Yankee marksmen then took careful aim and squeezed off shots. The redcoats fell like wooden soldiers.

Like a giant ribbon, the British column snaked up the road. The soldiers' flaming red jackets made perfect targets against the green background. Col-

onel Smith sent out flanking troops to try to flush
the Americans out of the woods before the main column marched by. But the flankers, too, were mowed
down by rifle fire. Nothing Colonel Smith did could
prevent the slaughter. British Lieutenant Barker
described the horror of the march: "We were fired
on from all sides. . . . The country was an amazingly
strong one, full of hills, woods, stone walls, etc.,
which the rebels did not fail to take advantage of,
for they were all lined with people who kept an
incessant fire upon us. . . . In this way we
marched. . . miles, their numbers increasing from all
parts, while ours was reducing by deaths, wounds,
and fatigue."

It took the British two hours to march the six
miles back to Lexington. To the troops, it seemed

like an eternity. Rifle balls whistled at them from every direction. The shots seemed to have been fired by invisible soldiers. When the British tried to return the fire, they found that their enemies had vanished into the forest. Upon reaching Lexington, the usually orderly British army had become a fleeing mob.

The redcoats were relieved to find reinforcements waiting for them in Lexington. Three crack regiments equipped with cannons had moved into the tiny town. The British command now passed to Lord Percy. To demonstrate the power of his forces, Percy ordered some of his cannons fired. One cannonball crashed into the east side of the Lexington meetinghouse and screamed out of the west side.

Before resuming the march, Lord Percy reinforced his flanker troops. He also issued new orders: kill all snipers and burn any house that harbors snipers. But Percy's measures did not stop the Americans. Along both sides of the road riflemen waited. British flankers broke into hundreds of houses near the road. Minutes earlier, those houses had been alive with American riflemen. But when the British entered, they were suddenly empty. Then, as soon as the British left, the houses again became a beehive of Minutemen. The British forces burned many rebel houses. But it was impossible to burn every house between Lexington and Boston.

At sunset, the exhausted British soldiers stumbled their last mile into Boston. In the city they were safe. Cannons from British warships covered the narrow approaches to Boston Harbor.

The unbelievable April day had at last come to an end. The splendid British army had been thoroughly frustrated by a ragged band of Americans. The British had lost 73 men killed, 174 wounded, and 26 missing. Almost 4,000 Americans had seen action by the end of the day. The Americans counted 49 killed, 39 wounded, and 5 missing. About the quality of American fighting men, Lord Percy wrote: "Whoever looks upon them as an irregular mob will find himself much mistaken."

Far more than just a battle had taken place. The fighting that broke out at the two Massachusetts towns changed the thinking of the colonists forever.

While the shots were being fired, American statesman Benjamin Franklin was sailing home from England. For ten years Franklin had been in Great Britain trying to iron out the differences between the colonies and the mother country. He

believed the Americans should have self-government. But he hoped they would remain united with Britain. Many colonists agreed with Franklin. They were not anxious to break their hundred-year-old ties with England. When news of Lexington and Concord swept the colonies, however, Americans began marching to a new drumbeat. Benjamin Franklin and others who once sought accord with the British now sought only independence. They continued seeking independence through a bitter war that lasted six and a half years.

After the bloodshed at Lexington and Concord, most Americans turned their thoughts to the words spoken a month earlier by the rebel Patrick Henry: "Is life so dear, or peace so sweet, as to be purchased at the price of chains and slavery? Forbid it, Almighty God! I know not what course others may take; but as for me, give me liberty, or give me death!"

About the Author

R. Conrad Stein was born and grew up in Chicago. He enlisted in the Marine Corps at the age of eighteen, and served for three years. He then attended the University of Illinois, where he received a Bachelor's Degree in history. He later studied in Mexico and earned a Master of Fine Arts degree from the University of Guanajuato.

The study of history is Mr. Stein's hobby. Since he finds it to be an exciting subject, he tries to bring the excitement of history to his readers. He is the author of many other books, articles, and short stories written for young people.

About the Artist

Keith Neely attended the School of the Art Institute of Chicago and received a Bachelor of Fine Arts degree with honors from the Art Center College of Design, where he majored in illustration. He has worked as an art director, designer, and illustrator and has taught advertising illustration and advertising design at Biola College in La Mirada, California. Mr. Neely is currently a freelance illustrator whose work has appeared in numerous magazines, books, and advertisements. He lives with his wife and five children in Flossmoor, Illinois, a suburb of Chicago.